CULTURE
in India

Melanie Guile

Raintree

Chicago, Illinois

For information, address the publisher:
Raintree, 100 N. LaSalle, Suite 1200, Chicago, IL 60602

Customer Service: 888-363-4266
Visit our website at www.raintreelibrary.com.

Printed in China by WKT Company Ltd.

09 08 07 06 05
10 9 8 7 6 5 4 3 2 1

Library of Congress Cataloging-in-Publication Data

Guile, Melanie.
  Culture in India / Melanie Guile.-- 1st ed.
     p. cm. -- (Culture in--)
  Includes bibliographical references and index.
  ISBN 1-4109-1134-9 (hb, library binding)
  1. India--Civilization--Juvenile literature. I. Title.   II. Series: Guile, Melanie. Culture in--
  DS423.G82 2005
  306'.0954--dc22

                                        2004016649

Acknowledgments
The publisher would like to thank the following for permission to reproduce photographs: AFP Photo: pp. 11, 23 (lower), 25, 28; Australian Picture Library/Corbis: pp. 13, 23 (upper), /Corbis/Michael Boys: p. 17; Dinodia Photo Library: pp. 8, 9, 10 (both), 19, 20, 21, 24, 26, 29; Getty Images/Aris Messinis/AFP: p. 18, /Robert Nickelsberg/Time Life Pictures: p. 15 (upper), /Prakash Singh/AFP: p. 15 (lower); Lonely Planet Images/Richard I'Anson: p. 27, /Liz Thompson: p. 12, /Eric Wheater: p. 7; Photolibrary.com: p. 16, /Index Stock: p. 14.

Cover photograph of Great Elephant Show reproduced with permission of Australian Picture Library/Corbis/Blaine Harrington III.

Every effort has been made to contact copyright holders of any material reproduced in this book. Any omissions will be rectified in subsequent printings if notice is given to the publishers.

The paper used to print this book comes from sustainable resources.

CONTENTS

Some words are shown in bold, **like this.** You can find out what they mean by looking in the glossary.

CULTURE IN
India

The great wedge of India hangs from the Asian continent between the Arabian Sea in the west and the Bay of Bengal in the east. Its position at the crossroads between Europe and Asia meant that waves of invaders swept through the country over thousands of years. They added their cultures to those of the **indigenous** tribal peoples, many of whom still survive in remote areas. All these different **ethnic groups** have left India with one of the world's richest cultures, dating back more than 5,000 years.

What Is Culture?

Culture is a people's way of living. It is the way in which people identify themselves as a group, separate and different from any other. Culture includes a group's spoken and written language, social customs, and habits, as well as its traditions of art, crafts, dance, drama, music, literature, and religion.

India's **diversity** of religions, languages, and cultures means there are thousands of smaller cultures flourishing within India. Government attempts to encourage a national focus have only partly succeeded, and in elections people still vote along **caste** and religious lines. Nevertheless, there are still many shared Indian values.

Throughout India, the family is the center of people's lives. Several generations of an extended family often live together, with men making the important decisions. Many families arrange important celebrations after consulting an astrological chart, called a *kundali,* to find the luckiest date.

The national religion, **Hinduism,** binds the majority of Indians together with common goals, duties, and rituals. Tolerance is also an important shared value in this **multicultural** country of more than a billion people.

Languages

More than 1,500 languages are spoken in India, and 18 are officially recognized. Hindi is spoken by twenty percent of the population and is the language of government. Other main languages are Bengali, Gujarati, Urdu, Punjabi, Tamil, and English. Hindi shares many similarities with **Sanskrit,** the ancient language of classical Indian literature.

4

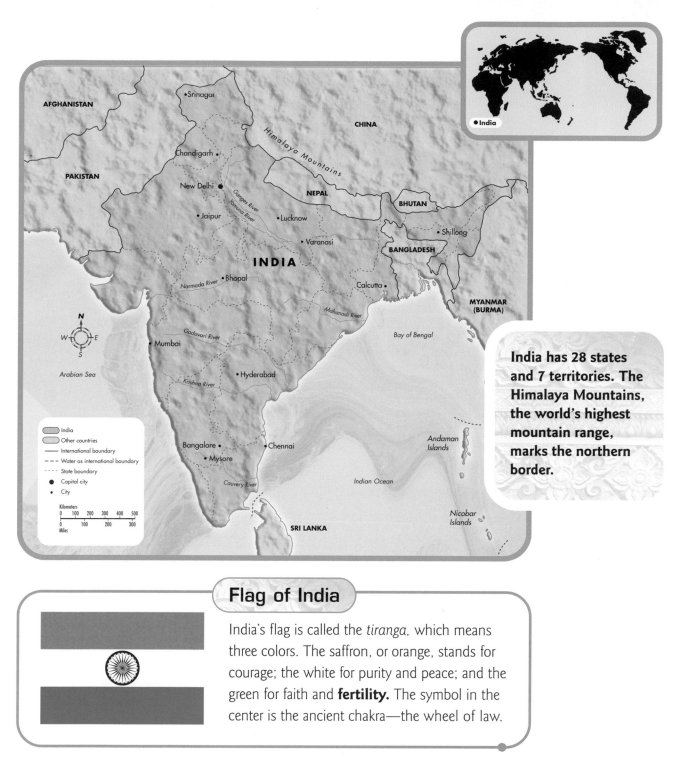

India has 28 states and 7 territories. The Himalaya Mountains, the world's highest mountain range, marks the northern border.

Flag of India

India's flag is called the *tiranga*, which means three colors. The saffron, or orange, stands for courage; the white for purity and peace; and the green for faith and **fertility.** The symbol in the center is the ancient chakra—the wheel of law.

Land of Extremes

India is a land of contrasts and extremes. Massive industrial growth and success in technology has brought great wealth to the top third of the population. There is also a growing Indian middle class, but 233 million people still have no education, no health care, and go to bed hungry every night. Although school is **compulsory** to the age of 14, only about 60 percent of children attend, and only about 60 percent of the population can read and write.

History

In about 2500 B.C.E., the people of the **Indus Valley** created great cities, pottery, and artwork in what is now Pakistan. Lighter-skinned people called Aryans from Central Asia overran this **civilization** in about 1500 B.C.E. They introduced the **Hindu** religion and its **caste system,** which divides people into classes. They also drove India's original inhabitants, the Dravidians, into the south.

The great Mauryan Empire rose in about 300 B.C.E., with Ashoka as its most famous emperor. He encouraged a new religion called **Buddhism,** which began in Nepal in about 500 B.C.E. About 1000 C.E., **Muslims** from the Middle East overran the north. Their religion still flourishes there. The **Mughals** invaded in 1526 and later built magnificent monuments, including the famous Taj Mahal in Agra. The British ruled India from the 1800s until Indian **independence** in 1947. They left behind English education, English legal systems, and cricket—India's most popular sport.

Partition

At the time of independence, Muslim areas in the north were **partitioned** off from India to form the new countries of Pakistan in the west and Bangladesh in the east. Although the aim was to reduce religious tension between Muslims and Hindus, disputes over borders and religious issues have often resulted in war between India and Pakistan.

Gandhi—Person of Peace

One of the world's great leaders, Mohandas Karamchand Gandhi, also known as Mahatma Gandhi (1869–1948), is best known for his idea of nonviolent protest. Born into a wealthy family, he championed the rights of the poor, particularly the Dalits—the untouchables. He fought for Indian independence from Great Britain through nonviolent protests such as hunger strikes and workers' strikes. Named Mahatma, meaning Great Soul, Gandhi was greatly loved, and all India mourned when he was **assassinated** in 1948.

The People

India has the world's second-largest population, with almost 1.05 billion people and 5,653 different **ethnic groups.** About 72 percent of people live in the country on farms. Hundreds of **indigenous** tribes live in remote communities outside the main culture. The average **life expectancy** is only 63 years. India is a **democracy,** and its prime minister is Shri Atal Bihari Vajpayee.

Religions

About 83 percent of Indians are Hindus. They worship many gods and goddesses, each a form of the supreme being, Brahman. Hindus believe in **reincarnation.** This means being reborn as something either better or worse, depending on the deeds—called karma—in your current life. Lower castes and Dalits, or untouchables, cannot achieve *moksha,* which is the freedom from rebirth. Doing your duty, known as dharma, means studying the holy texts called the Vedas, making temple offerings, becoming a holy person known as a sadhu, and bathing in the Ganges River. These are ways of improving your chances of achieving *moksha.*

Muslims make up twelve percent of the population and live mainly in the north. Although there has often been tension between Muslims and Hindus, for the most part they live together peacefully. Other religious groups include **Sikhs, Christians,** and **Jains.** The Himalayan states of the far north are mostly Buddhist.

TRADITIONS
and Customs

With such a rich culture, Indians have learned to live with contrasts. **Sacred** cows that, according to **Hindu** custom, must be allowed to roam free, graze on the edge of six-lane freeways. Farmers plow with animals beside cutting-edge technology factories.

Mosques, temples, *gurudwaras,* and churches exist side-by-side. Top women executives still wear red *bindis,* a spot on the forehead, which stands for *shakti,* or female energy. Great leaders such as Gandhi and Jawaharlal Nehru, independent India's first prime minister, united the people in peaceful nationhood. Indians are proud of belonging to the world's largest **democracy.** Nevertheless, deep divisions persist.

India is a place of extremes, with old and new existing side-by-side.

The Caste System

All Hindus are born into a **caste** that dictates where they live, who they can marry, and the jobs they can do. Castes are ranked from Brahmins (traditionally priests) at the top, through Kshatriyas (warriors), Vaishyas (merchants), and Shudras (servants or workers) at the bottom. The top three castes, called the twice-born, are permitted to read the sacred Hindu texts, or Vedas, but Shudras are not. Below these ranks are the untouchables, called Dalits, which means broken ones. People cannot change their caste and often must marry within it. Although laws have been passed to outlaw the caste system, most believe the laws have been ineffective.

Despite laws to protect them, Dalits still suffer **discrimination**.

Great Dalit Leader

Dr. Bhimrao Ramji Ambedkar, born a Dalit, became a lawyer and fought for justice and equality for all castes. He rose to become the minister for law. He single-handedly drafted the Indian **constitution,** which guarantees Dalits seats in Parliament, the right to attend college, and government jobs.

Dalits

Dalits make up twenty percent of India. Labeled as polluted in ancient Hindu texts, they were denied education and restricted to the worst jobs. Higher-caste Hindus would not touch or mix with them. Untouchability was banned in 1950, and laws were passed to favor Dalits. However, most still do not own land, at least 50 percent live in poverty, only about 40 percent can read and write, and their average life expectancy is 42 years, more than 20 years lower than that of other Indians.

Women and Girls

Women usually come second to men in Indian society. Women are often expected to obey and serve their husbands and sons and to work many more hours than men. Girls are often seen as burdens because huge **dowries** must be paid by their families when they marry. Male babies are celebrated because they will later take care of the family. Although these attitudes are officially discouraged, and educated men and women speak out against them, some women try to stop their pregnancies if they know they are carrying a girl. This has led to more boys than girls being born, at 100 males to every 93 females.

On the other hand, since 1993 one-third of local government seats have been set aside for women. This has greatly increased their involvement in politics. In 1966, India elected one of the world's first female prime ministers, Indira Gandhi.

Hindu Marriage

Most **Hindu** marriages are arranged by the parents of the intended couple, although young women can refuse the match. The couple must have the same star sign according to the *janam kundali,* or horoscope, and a **dowry** may be set. At an engagement ceremony, the groom's family gives the bride a wedding sari, which is a kind of dress. The wedding itself is held under a canopy, where the couple have their feet washed, join hands, and exchange flower wreaths. They then walk around a **sacred** fire seven times chanting prayers in a ritual called the *saptapadi.* Guests throw rice and flower petals for wealth and happiness.

Hindu marriage ceremonies include numerous **rituals**. The traditional red sari is worn to bring good luck.

Religious Festivals

With so many different cultural groups, festivals fill the calendar. **Buddhists** in the Himalayan states of Sikkim and Himachal Pradesh celebrate *Buddha Jayanti,* usually in May or June. This event celebrates the birth and **enlightenment** of Lord Buddha. **Christians** fill the churches during Christmas and Easter. Individual Hindu gods and goddesses have their own special days, like the *Ganesh Chaturthi* festival in August or September. It honors the popular elephant-headed god of luck and success, Ganesh.

At *Ganesh Chaturthi*, Hindus pray to the god Ganesh for good luck and happiness.

Festival of Lights

Deepavali or *Divali,* the Festival of Lights in October or November, is the most important Hindu festival. Families clean their houses, buy new clothes, and gather to celebrate the New Year. Little clay lamps called *diyas* are lit to welcome the goddess of wealth, Lakshmi, into the home. Fairy lights are also hung in city streets. Special sticky sweets called *halva* and *coconut burfi* are eaten, and gifts are exchanged.

Holi

Holi in February or March is a spring festival to worship Lord Krishna. The night before, Hindus make temple offerings during the *puja* ritual and afterward light a huge bonfire. But most people enjoy the fun part of *Holi.* This involves throwing colored water or colored powder called *gulal* over everyone in sight. Many people end up covered with different colors and soaking wet. At noon the fun stops, and people go home to wash and change.

Id-ul-Fitr

Id-ul-Fitr means "feast of the breaking of the fast" and is the most important festival for **Muslims.** It marks the end of the 30-day fasting period of Ramzan, or Ramadan, in the ninth month of the Muslim calendar. During this time, Muslims do not eat or drink from sunrise to sunset. Families attend mosque early, dress in new clothes, and give money and food to charity. Afterward, there is lots of eating and visiting with family and friends.

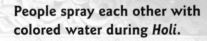

People spray each other with colored water during *Holi*.

Toda Rituals

The **indigenous** Toda people worship nature and the buffalo. They celebrate a baby's birth by presenting it to the sacred buffalo at a naming ceremony. The baby's head is shaved, and its face is uncovered for the first time. It is then displayed to the dairy herd. Female babies are fed buttermilk. Male babies have their heads touched at the dairy door.

MINORITY GROUPS

With about 635 different tribes, India has the world's largest number of **indigenous** people, who are called *adivasis. Adivasis* make up about eight percent of the population and include the ancient bowpeople called the Bhils, the tribal Santhals, the Toda of Tamil Nadu, and the coastal Halakkis.

A young Bhil groom prepares for a wedding ceremony.

Below even the Dalits in the **Hindu caste system,** *adivasis* are India's most disadvantaged people. Despite many laws to help them, **discrimination,** a lack of educational opportunities, and the loss of land threaten their ways of life.

The Santhals and the Bhils

The Santhals are India's largest tribal group, numbering around ten million. Concentrated in the eastern and central states, they were originally forest-dwelling farmers. However, in the 1900s many **migrated** to work in the tea plantations of Assam and West Bengal. Today, most Santhals work in quarrying and laboring jobs and are among the poorest people in the country.

Around one million Bhils live in central India. Originally hunters with a reputation of being fond of war and battle, today they live in small farming communities under a headperson called the *tadvi.* Most Bhil are Hindu, but some also worship stone images and the spirits of the forest. Traditional Bhil weddings are very costly and include up to 50 separate **rituals.** In one, animal and human figures are drawn on the walls of the bridal hut, and the couple walks seven times counterclockwise around a **sacred** pole.

The Toda

The Toda of Tamil Nadu are an ancient forest hill tribe who worship the buffalo. Strict vegetarians, the Toda live off the milk their cattle produce and the butter they make from it. They build striking, cone-shaped shrines in which the men worship and have important songs and rituals based on the buffalo. The women are skilled at embroidering the famous Toda shawls, which have sacred meaning. Only about 1,000 Toda survive today, and their culture is quickly disappearing.

The Halakki Farmers

Unlike many *adivasis,* the Halakkis live on the outskirts of towns on the southwest coast. About 75,000 Halakkis live in thatched mud huts decorated with **abstract** wall paintings known as *hali.* The women, called *gowdathis,* are famous for the masses of necklaces and other jewelry they wear. During the *Holi* festival, the men perform a harvest dance, called a *suggi kunita,* wearing special costumes. These include a red and yellow *kurta pyjama* and a lavish headpiece called a *turayi* made of flowers, beads, and paper. The men also carry a bunch of peacock feathers, or *kuncha,* and drumsticks known as *kolu* as they dance in a circle to singing and the beat of drums.

Ghotuls—Forest Schools

Tribal people all over central India have an education system that dates back thousands of years. Jungle schools called *ghotuls* are run by the young people. All aspects of tribal living are taught, including leaf weaving, wood carving, singing, and dancing. Married people are not allowed into the schools, and young children learn from older ones.

COSTUMES
and Clothing

According to ancient Indian beliefs, unstitched cloth is more pure, so many Indian costumes are simply lengths of material wrapped around the head or body. Their beauty comes from the brilliant colors, the different weaves, and the decorations on the fabrics, many of which are still handwoven and embroidered by village people.

Traditional Clothing

Women everywhere wear traditional clothes, and fashion designers bring out new versions each year.

The national dress of Indian women is the sari. It is made of a twenty-foot (six-meter) length of material, usually with an embroidered or woven border. It is worn with a blouse and a long drawstring undergarment. Saris are wrapped to form a graceful, long dress with the tail, called the decorated *pallu,* draped over the shoulder.

The *salwar kameez* is worn all over northern India. A flowing tunic dress, or *kameez,* is worn over loose pants drawn tight at the ankles. A light scarf, or *dupatta,* is draped around the neck and often covers the head.

Traditional men's clothing is simple. It is a piece of cloth wrapped around the waist called a *lungi* or a length of material wrapped around the hips and between the legs to form pants called *dhoti.* The *kurta pyjama* consists of a long shirt and loose white pants. However, aside from farmworkers, few Indian men wear traditional clothing today, preferring Western-style shirts and pants.

The graceful sari is the oldest recorded traditional costume in the world.

The Language of Gold

Indian women wear their wealth in the form of jewelry. Gold was thought to purify the skin and is still very popular. Bangles are believed to protect the wearer, and a nose stud is a symbol of purity. A special necklace called a *mangalasutra* is worn as a wedding token, and toe rings and anklets are worn mainly by married women.

The *pheta* is a huge turban made of twenty feet (six meters) of cloth.

Sikh men wear turbans, consisting of a long piece of plain material wrapped tightly around the head. In Rajasthan and Maharashtra, men wear a *pheta,* a roll of cloth wound in **intricate** folds to form a huge turban.

Folk Costumes

Brilliant colors and gleaming mirrorwork embroidery are favored by the women of Rajasthan and Gujarat. They wear long, pleated skirts called *ghaghras* or *lehengas,* teamed with backless blouses called *cholis* and cotton scarfs called *dupattas.* Both are elaborately embroidered. Chunky bangles, earrings, and anklets complete the *ghaghra choli* outfit.

Indian Fashion Industry

Indian designers are famous for their luxurious fabrics and glamorous styles. Leading designer Rohit Bal was called "India's master of fabric and fantasy" by *Time* magazine. His 2003 collection featured embroidered men's jackets and traditional *lungi* with zippers and leather belts.

Even better known is Ritu Kumar, who brought traditional, handmade fabrics to high fashion. Among her famous clients was the late Princess Diana. Kumar also makes the gowns for Miss India in beauty pageants.

Gowns by Ritu Kumar are in demand around the world.

FOOD

India is the home of hot, spicy food, much of which is vegetarian. Dozens of different spices are used in cooking, including chili, cloves, coriander, cumin, cardamom, and turmeric. These are freshly ground and fried to bring out the rich flavors. They are then cooked with vegetables, lamb, fish, or chicken to make spicy stews. Rice accompanies almost every meal and is the staple, or basic food, in southern India. In the north, different types of breads are eaten as well.

Originally from the south, _thali_ is now eaten throughout India.

South Indian Food

Most meals in the south are rice-based. A very common dish is _thali,_ which is often served on a large banana leaf. It consists of a mound of boiled white rice with curried vegetables. Small side dishes of yogurt, chutney, pickles, and sometimes a tasty **lentil** stew called _dhal_ go with the rice. Small snacks are usually eaten for breakfast. These include _idli,_ which is rice and lentil cakes steamed and served with a thick tomato and lentil sauce called _sambar_ and coconut chutney. _Pongal,_ a dish of spiced sticky rice, is also a popular breakfast meal.

Food in the North

More meat is eaten in northern India, reflecting the influence of the **Mughals** who occupied the area for about 200 years (1526–1707). They introduced the _tandoor,_ a clay oven for slow cooking to bring out subtle flavors. Tandoori chicken is soaked in herbs and yogurt before cooking and is famously tender. _Biryani_ consists of meat mixed with spicy rice and dried fruits. Kababs—meat threaded on to skewers and grilled—are also popular in the north. Lamb, chicken, and fish are eaten, but pork is forbidden to **Muslims. Hindus** also do not eat beef because the cow is **sacred** to them.

Wheat is grown in the colder north, so bread is baked there, either in the _tandoor_ or on a hot plate called a roti or chapati. _Parathas_ are breads cooked in butter and often stuffed with curried potatoes and vegetables. Puffed-up, crisp _pappadams_ are deep-fried lentil flour wafers and are popular around the world.

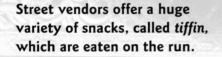

Street vendors offer a huge variety of snacks, called *tiffin*, which are eaten on the run.

Finger Food

People throughout India eat with their fingers, but there is a knack to it. Only the right hand is used because the left is considered unclean. Food is scooped into little mounds and carried up to the mouth with the four fingers, then the thumb shovels the food into the mouth. Only the thumb touches the lips, leaving the other fingers clean to return to the plate. It is considered impolite to dirty your fingers beyond the second joints.

Meals on Wheels

Office workers in the city of Mumbai do not have to put up with boring cold lunches. Many people cook three-course hot meals and put them in lunch boxes called *dabbas*. Delivery people called *dabbawallahs* pick them up, deliver them to the offices, and return the containers afterward. Although most *dabbawallahs* cannot read, markings on the *dabbas* help them identify the boxes. *Dabbawallahs* are found only in Mumbai. The trade is dying out due to the increasing number of working couples and the fact that many businesspeople do not have time to eat elaborate midday meals.

PERFORMING ARTS

In India, music, dance, and drama began as a form of Hindu temple worship. The basics of the classical style were written down by Bharata Muni around 2,000 years ago in a book called the *Natya Shastra*. This text has shaped traditional Indian music ever since.

Traditional Music

Indian classical music uses quartertones and sliding scales to create a flowing, multilayered sound. There are two main types—Hindustani from northern India and Carnatic from the south—but they share many common features. Usually the rhythm, or tala, is beaten out by a drum, and the background drone or hum comes from bass instruments. A singer or main instrument creates the raga, or melody. Singers are highly skilled and **improvise** around the ragas, which convey different moods.

Instruments

Traditional stringed instruments can be played with a bow, but most are plucked. The sitar is a long-necked, guitarlike instrument usually with seventeen strings, plus "sympathetic strings" inside the neck that vibrate to give a magical, echoing sound. The ancient vina from southern India is like a large mandolin with two ball-shaped echo chambers attached to the neck.

Sitar master Ravi Shankar introduced this classical instrument to the West when he taught George Harrison of the Beatles to play it in the 1960s.

Twin drums called tabla commonly set the beat. On the skins is a black spot made of gum, soot, and iron filings, which makes a bell-like sound when struck. Clappers, cymbals, and large drums are also used. Bamboo flutes called *bansuri* are popular. The flute used by snake charmers is called a *pungi*. It consists of two tubes attached to a hollowed-out coconut that contains vibrating reeds. It makes an eerie sound when blown. Traditional orchestras generally consist of five or six players and accompany classical singers.

Modern Sounds

Bhangra is a modern fusion of Indian folk music with rap, reggae, and rhythm and blues. Based on Punjabi folk music with its wild drum rhythms, it is popular in dance clubs in Europe and Asia. Punjabi singer-songwriter Daler Mehndi is known in India as the king of *bhangra*. He used modern Western instruments and lyrics along with *bhangra* folk traditions in his 1995 smash hit album *Bolo Ta Ra Ra*. Daler Mehndi's upbeat songs and rich voice along with his jeweled turban have won him international fame.

Indipop

About 70 percent of albums sold in India are songs from movies made in Mumbai—often called **Bollywood.** Soundtracks blend Indian classical music with a folksy flavor, and singers have huge followings.

But Indian pop music was unknown until singer Alisha Chinai released her *Made in India* album in 1994. She mixed Western pop sounds with traditional Indian music to create Indipop, which swept the country. Today, Indipop is extremely popular. There is even an all-woman band called Viva, whose members were handpicked by a national television station.

Classical Drama

Dance, music, and storytelling come together in the ancient dance-drama known as the *kutiyattam*. Originally performed only in temples, the drama begins with an actor called a *chakyar* addressing the audience in the ancient **Sanskrit** language. Characters wear makeup and elaborate costumes and use mime, voice, and a group of drummers to tell religious stories.

Classical Dance

Kathak, from northern India, is a blend of ancient dance-drama and **Muslim** influences. The performers use mime and dance to relate **Hindu epic** tales. The dance includes rapid spins and foot-stamping, and dancers wear ankle bells that jingle as they move. *Kathak* was usually danced by women and accompanied by traditional instruments.

The *bharata natyam* comes from the southern state of Tamil Nadu and is one of the oldest dances in India. Female dancers called *devadasis* traditionally lived in Hindu temples and handed down their skills to their daughters. Graceful movements and facial expressions convey emotions in this carefully controlled dance of jumps, spins, and balanced poses.

Very different in mood is the energetic men's dance called the *kathakali*, which comes from Kerala in southern India. The men wear green face makeup, large gold headdresses, and swinging robes. They perform spectacular, all-night dances in the open air, accompanied by a traditional orchestra of tabla, strings, and flutes.

The classical solo dance, *bharata natyam*, from southern India, uses hand gestures called *mudras* and facial expressions to convey emotions.

Men perform the *bhangra*
dance at a festival in Punjab.

Folk Dance

Apart from classical dances, smaller
communities of people also had folk
dances to celebrate important events. The
chhau from Orissa began as a martial art.
Masked dancers leap and spin, often using
swords or shields with great skill. In the
Punjab area, the *bhangra* developed as a
harvest festival dance. Lively movements are
accompanied by singing and the rapid beat
of the *dhol* drum and *chimta,* or metal
clappers. The *bhangra* gave its name to a
popular form of modern music based on
the raw energy of the dance.

Puppet Theater

Puppet theater was invented in India
more than 1,000 years ago. All puppet
forms are found there, including
stringed **marionettes,** rod puppets,
and finger puppets. Flat leather
"shadow puppets" are worked by rods
and strings from behind a lit screen.
The life-sized figures are made of
dyed and **intricately** carved goatskin
and glow with color when the light
shines through them.

LITERATURE

Literature has been an important part of India's culture for thousands of years, and some of the world's oldest works were written there. Today's internationally successful writers continue that tradition.

Ancient Literature

The great **Hindu** holy books, the Vedas, were written in about 1500–1200 B.C.E. The first book, the *Rig Veda,* has 1,028 verses of creation stories and prayers and is written in the ancient **Sanskrit** language. The Vedas are regarded as the word of god and form the basis of the Hindu religion.

Hindu Epic Tales

Begun in about 1000 B.C.E., the *Mahabharata* is a collection of stories, including descriptions of the heroic deeds of the Hindu god Krishna and his battles against evil demons. It is the world's largest work of literature.

Even better known is the *Ramayana.* It was written in about 300 B.C.E. by Valmiki, a robber turned singer-poet. Written in Sanskrit verse, the *Ramayana* tells of the god Rama's love for the beautiful Sita. The story tells how he saved her from the villain Ravana with the help of Hanuman, the mischievous monkey-god. Today, tales from the *Ramayana* are retold in traditional drama and puppet performances. A 78-part television series based on it brought all of India to a stop every Sunday during 1987 and 1988.

Sanskrit Master

India's greatest Sanskrit writer, Kalidasa, lived in about 350–400 C.E. He wrote only three plays and four poems but is greatly admired for his realistic characters and the beauty of his language. His masterpiece is a poem of 111 verses titled *Meghaduuta.* It describes a man who, separated from his wife, writes of the sad beauty of the landscape and his feelings of loss.

Man of Malgudi

R. K. Narayan (1906–2001) is India's best-loved writer in English. He created the imaginary town Malgudi that became the setting for many stories, including the famous *Malgudi Days* and *Under the Banyan Tree.* His charming descriptions of ordinary people and everyday life won him many awards around the world.

World Poet

Rabindranath Tagore was born in Calcutta in 1861.

Legendary writer Rabindranath Tagore (1861–1941) wrote plays, stories, and poetry. His book of poems, *Geetanjali,* caused a sensation in London, and in 1913 he won the Nobel Prize for Literature. Tagore was also a painter, teacher, and musician and wrote the Indian national anthem, "*Jana Gana Mana,*" which means "Thou Art the Ruler of All Minds."

Arundhati Roy won the Booker Prize for her novel *The God of Small Things.*

Literature Today

India has produced a host of internationally renowned writers. Vikram Seth received high praise for his novel *A Suitable Boy* (1993), which was a family saga full of lively and unusual characters. Arundhati Roy wrote the novel *The God of Small Things*, for which she won the Booker Prize in 1997. It explores the evils of the **caste system** through the lives of two children.

Ruth Prawer Jhabvala was born in Germany into a Jewish family but lived in India for many years. She wrote nine novels, including the Booker Prize–winning *Heat and Dust*. She has also won two Academy Awards for her film scripts *A Room with a View* in 1985 and *Howards End* in 1992.

Anita Desai is famous for her novels, including *Fire on the Mountain* (1977) and the award-winning children's book *The Village by the Sea* (1982). Her daughter, Kiran Desai, wrote the international best-seller *Hullabaloo in the Guava Orchard* (1998).

FILM
and Television

India has the world's largest film industry, with audiences in the hundreds of millions and big-budget studios. Television is also extremely popular, and Indian people generally prefer locally produced programs.

Film Pioneers

In 1913, Dadasaheb Phalke (1870–1944) screened his first movie, *Raja Harishchandra*, based on an Indian **epic** tale. His studio near Bombay made about 95 silent movies before "talkies," or movies with sound, put him out of business. The first sound film screened in India was *Alam Ara* (1931) by director Ardershir Irani. It featured seven songs, and musical numbers have been a part of Indian blockbuster movies ever since.

Golden Era of Film

The 1950s saw the rise of filmmaker Satyajit Ray, who is regarded as one of the world's great directors. Ray created realistic, moving stories about ordinary people. His famous first film, *Pather Panchali* (*Song of the Road*, 1955), about a poor village boy named Apu, is now a classic. Ray was awarded an Oscar for Lifetime Achievement shortly before he died in 1992.

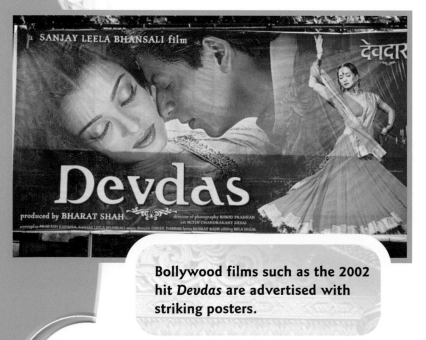

Bollywood films such as the 2002 hit *Devdas* are advertised with striking posters.

Bollywood

Lavish costumes and sets, unlikely plots, and glamorous stars are all found in the popular movies made in the Mumbai (previously called Bombay) studios known as **Bollywood.** Called "*masala* movies" because they include a bit of everything—like *masala* spice mix—the films combine fantasy, singing, dancing, violence, and romance.

Singing Superstar

He was short, plain, and balding, but Kundan Lal Saigal (1904–1947) was India's first film star. Acting during the 1930s and 1940s, his brilliant voice and striking looks suited tragic hero roles in which he sang, danced, and wore a wig to hide his thinning hair.

Bollywood star Madhuri Dixit hosts the popular reality television show *Kahin naa Kahin koi hai*.

Star Attractions

Shah Rukh Khan is one of India's top movie stars. He made his debut in 1988 in the TV hit series *Fauji*, a soap about a group of military trainees. Although critics dislike his overdramatic style, moviegoers love him. He starred in the Bollywood remake of the tragic love epic *Devdas* in 2002, the most expensive Indian film ever made. His costar was former Miss World, Aishwarya Rai, India's hottest Bollywood actress.

International Impact

Bombay-born producer-director Ismail Merchant and American partner James Ivory have won high praise for their fine **adaptations** of English classic novels. Actor turned writer-director Mira Nair's sensitive first feature, *Salaam Bombay!* (1988), won 26 awards and is regarded as a classic. Her 2000 feature, *Monsoon Wedding*, was also an international success. London-raised Gurinder Chadha achieved a hit with her crosscultural movie *Bend It Like Beckham* (2002) about a **Sikh** girl in England who wants to play soccer. In 2003, Chadha found success overeas, as a medical student on NBC's *E.R.*

Television

About 80 percent of people in India have a television. The government owns and controls some stations, and private satellite TV is growing. Local versions of American dramas, sitcoms, and game shows are popular. The top soap is *Kyunki Saas Bhi Kabhi Bahu Thi*, a Cinderella-style comedy-drama about three nasty aunts-in-law and their long-suffering *bahu,* or daughter/niece-in-law Tulsi. Reality TV became popular in 2002 with *Kahin naa Kahin koi hai* ("There is someone out there"), a show that arranges marriages on the spot for young singles. It is hosted by top film actress Madhuri Dixit.

ARTS AND CRAFTS

Pottery statues found in the **Indus Valley** in modern-day Pakistan show that uniquely Indian art styles existed 5,000 years ago. Over the centuries, the skills of artists and artisans were refined, and today modern masters create a huge variety of arts and crafts.

The Ajanta Cave Paintings

For 800 years, from about 200 B.C.E., the monks at Ajanta painted scenes from the lives of the **Buddha** on the walls of their monastery caves. Today, the Ajanta cave paintings are world famous for the beauty and detail of the figures. The rock walls were coated with hair and clay plaster, painted with natural dyes, and polished to a sheen with stone. To this day, artists regard the Ajanta paintings as the best in Indian art, and many modern works are based on them.

Buddhist monks created the Ajanta cave paintings over a period of 800 years.

Stone Masterpieces

In about 300 B.C.E., the great Buddhist emperor Ashoka encouraged the arts and ordered great monuments to be built. One is the famous **Stupa** of Sanchi, in Madhya Pradesh. Built from stone-covered brick, the stupa marks a sacred place for Buddhists but is best known for the huge stone pillar topped with a carving of four lions. This ancient design was chosen as the emblem of the new India at **independence** in 1947. Four huge stone gateways, or *toranas,* were added in the 100s B.C.E. to represent the four corners of the universe. Made by ivory carvers, the gates are covered with finely detailed animals and human figures, including elephants, monkeys, and scenes from the life of the Buddha.

Folk Art

For centuries, Indian women have decorated the walls of their houses with patterns or pictures. In the state of Bihar, animals, goddesses, and scenes of village life were painted in bold, simple designs. Known as *mithila* paintings, they were originally done to bless the marriage chamber. Women used household spices as colors and applied them with bamboo twigs. Since the 1960s, the strong, simple designs have been created on paper and sold to collectors.

Kalighat paintings called *pats* were originally made as souvenirs for holy pilgrims to the Kali Temple in Calcutta. They were simple watercolor sketches of Hindu gods done by **anonymous** artists, called *patua,* to earn extra money. Subjects were often humorous and were depicted in bold colors and lively styles. *Pats* were created from about 1830 to 1930, after which printed images took over, but they are highly regarded by collectors today.

Framed prints of Hindu gods are displayed for sale at a market stall outside the Kali Temple.

The Black Pagoda

The Sun Temple of Konarak was built about 1250 C.E. from black sandstone. Its tall roof is covered with sculptures of female musicians welcoming the sun god as he travels across the sky. Aruna, the Lord of Dawn, is shown driving his huge chariot led by seven stone horses. A large sculpture of the god Surya is carved out of green stone in glowing contrast to the black temple.

The Birth of Modern Art

By the 1900s, Indian artists were looking for new ways to express themselves. In Calcutta, the famous Tagore family established the Bengal School. Here, artists broke away from European styles and produced new, uniquely Indian modern art, influenced by ancient painting traditions. Nandalal Bose (1883–1966) is the most famous of this group of artists. He painted traditional subjects such as village life and **Hindu** myths using simple folk-art techniques. Many regard him as India's best modern artist.

Modern Masters

India's most famous modern artist is Maqbool Fida Husain (1915–). He started out painting movie advertising billboards but soon gained recognition for his striking, **controversial** artwork. In his oil paintings, he uses bold colors and strong brushstrokes and is a master at showing moods and feelings. Later works include the *Shwetambari* exhibition, which featured sheet-covered walls and hundreds of shredded newspapers. In one public performance, he destroyed six of his works by painting over them in white. Husain is also a respected filmmaker.

Painter Amrita Sher-Gil (1913–1941) has a cult following, though she was born in Hungary and died at the age of 28. She is best known for her moody, intense portraits of women and was strongly influenced by her French art training. Her works have been declared National Art Treasures by the Indian government.

Modern artist M. F. Husain's **abstract** works are praised around the world.

Textiles

In villages all over India, people still weave cotton or silk cloth and dye or embroider it to make textiles. Varanasi is an important center of silk weaving. *Kinkab* is made there. This **brocade** is woven with gold or silver threads to make **intricate** patterns. A Varanasi *tanchoi sari* is covered with intricate flowers and birds.

Block printing is thought to have been invented in southern India and is still very popular. A piece of wood is carved in raised patterns, then dipped in dye before being stamped on plain cloth. Clothing, bedspreads, and tablecloths are commonly made this way for the international market. Another common technique is tie-dyeing. Here, the plain cloth is tightly knotted, then dipped into vats of dye. The undyed parts within the knots form swirling, abstract patterns.

Tarkashi silver work is made by looping silver wire into delicate patterns.

Heavenly Fabrics

The silk weavers of Varanasi give the patterns of their cloth charming names. An all-over pattern of silver thread is called *mazchar*, meaning "ripples of silver." *Chand tara*, woven in gold and silver, means "moon and stars."

Metalwork

Some of the world's finest metalwork comes from India. In Orissa, silver is stretched into fine wire and threaded to make delicate filigree work called *tarkashi*. The lacelike effect is used for jewelry, bags, and ornamental boxes. This ancient craft dates back more than 1,000 years. *Bidri* is a metalwork technique that originated in Iran. Copper and zinc is cast into bowls, urns, or plates, then patterns are etched or scratched into the blackened surface. Silver or gold leaf is then beaten into the grooves to create shining contrasts.

Looking to the Future

The rich variety of India's arts and crafts is a reflection of the country's complex and diverse culture. India continues to embrace new ideas as it moves with confidence through the 2000s. It is certain to remain one of the world's most vibrant cultures.

GLOSSARY

abstract not realistic or not easy to understand

adaptation reworking or new version

anonymous by an unknown author

assassinate to murder, usually for political reasons

Bollywood name for the studios in Mumbai (formerly Bombay) that make many popular Indian movies

brocade woven fabric with raised pattern

Buddhism religion in which followers study the teachings of the Buddha and strive for a peaceful state called enlightenment. A follower of Buddhism is a Buddhist.

caste system ancient Indian system that separates people into higher and lower classes

Christianity religion based on the belief in one God and the teachings of Jesus, as written in a holy book called the Bible. A follower of Christianity is called a Christian.

civilization state in an advanced stage of development

compulsory required, usually by law

constitution set of written rules by which a country is governed

controversial attracting criticism and argument

democracy form of government in which decisions are made by the people

discriminate to treat people unfairly on the basis of their race, gender, or religion, or for some other reason

diverse various kinds or forms

dowry money or goods that must be paid to the husband and family of a bride

enlightenment condition of spiritual peace and understanding

epic long traditional story about gods and heroes

ethnic group people who share a specific culture, language, and background

fertility fruitfulness

gesture movement of the body, usually the limbs

gurudwara Sikh palce of worship

Hinduism diverse religion that originated in India. Followers worship many gods and goddesses and believe in the rebirth of souls into new bodies after death. A follower of Hinduism is a Hindu.

improvise to make up spontaneously

independent free from foreign ruke

indigenous original or native to a particular country or area

Indus Valley valley of the Indus River, which now flows through Pakistan

intricate finely worked or complicated

Jainism Indian religion founded around 550 B.C.E. that teaches detachment from the world and avoiding injury to all living things. A follower is called a Jain.

lentil type of pulse, or seed, that is high in protein

life expectancy number of years a person can expect to live

marionette a doll-like puppet with movable arms and legs worked by strings from above

migrate to move permanently to a new area or country

Mughal Mongolian people from Central Asia whose leaders overran northern India and set up an empire there

multicultural made up of several different races and cultures

Muslim having to do with or following Islam, a religion based on belief in one god called Allah. Muslims follow the teachings of the prophet Mohammed, as written in a holy book called the Qu'ran.

partitioned separated into two countries

reincarnation belief that humans are reborn after death

ritual traditional religious or spiritual ceremony

sacred holy or religious

Sanskrit ancient written language of India, distantly related to English

Sikhism religion founded about 500 years ago and based in the Punjab area in northern India. It combines aspects of Islam and Hinduism. A follower is called a Sikh.

stupa mound or monument built over the ashes of important people, Buddhist monks, or relics

INDEX

DATE DUE

FEB 14 20